Carding, Spinning, Dyeing

An introduction to the traditional wool and flax crafts

Elisabeth Hoppe
Ragnar Edberg

Van Nostrand Reinhold Company
New York Cincinnati Toronto London Melbourne

Picture on front cover: spinning wheel from the year 1897; wool
yarn, and flax yarn, spun and dyed as described in the book

Van Nostrand Reinhold Company Regional Offices:
New York   Cincinnati   Chicago   Millbrae   Dallas

Van Nostrand Reinhold Company International Offices:
London   Toronto   Melbourne

This book was originally published in Swedish under the title
Karda, spinna, färga by ICA-forlaget AB, Vasteras, Sweden
Copyright © for *Karda, spinna, färga* by ICA-forlaget AB, Vasteras,
1973; English translation copyright © Van Nostrand Reinhold
Company Ltd., 1975

Translated from the Swedish by Marianne Turner

Library of Congress Catalog Card Number: 74-6790
ISBN: 0-442-30072-7
ISBN: 0-442-30073-5 (pbk)

This book is set in Optima and is printed in Great Britain
by Jolly and Barber Ltd., Rugby, Warwickshire

Published by Van Nostrand Reinhold Inc., 450 West 33rd Street,
New York, N.Y. 10001 and Van Nostrand Reinhold Co. Ltd.,
Molly Millar's Lane, Wokingham, Berkshire

16 15 14 13 12 11 10 9 8 7 6 5 4 3 2 1

Library of Congress Cataloging in Publication Data
Hoppe, Elisabeth, 1915–
Carding, spinning, dyeing.

Translation of Karda, spinna, farga.
Bibliography: p.
1. Hand spinning.   2. Carding.   3. Dyes and
dyeing.   I. Edberg, Ragnar, 1931–   joint author.
II. Title.
TT847.H6613   746   74-6790
ISBN 0-442-30072-7
ISBN 0-442-30073-5 pbk.

Contents

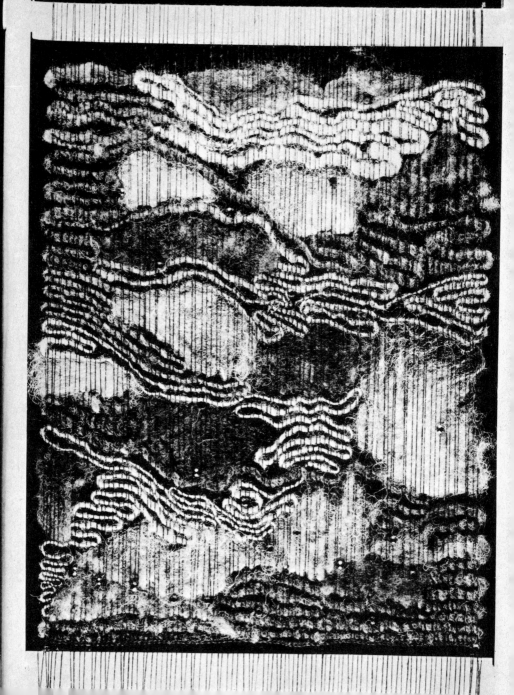

Introduction

During this century our society has changed rapidly and drastically. Farms, which at one time were alive with people and in close proximity to each other, now stand empty in winter time; the friendly rural life has been exchanged for the isolation of identical flats in tall city buildings.

The drift from country to town has meant breaking with many old traditions. Skills which had been handed down from father to son are now forgotten. New generations learnt new techniques, and new materials entered into our way of life. There were many improvements – life has become more comfortable, less exacting – but there is much that we could well do without, and there are many things whose passing we regret.

When each community was self-supporting, it was a necessity to know about the treatment of wool and flax in order to make clothes for everyday wear and festive occasions. Often, work in these materials was developed into a fine art. There are many of us who wish to preserve this tradition and to create works of art for our own pleasure and the enjoyment of others. Articles of wool and linen are no longer made to serve practical purposes alone, but increasingly bear the stamp of creative art.

The wider the gap between former generations, who knew the skills, and our own, the greater the risk that these crafts will be forgotten. For most of us it was our great-grandmother who knew the secret of how to deal with wool and flax. Here, we have collected some of the facts which she was unable to pass on, in order that the knowledge may be preserved. We hope that this book will prove a useful guide for the reader and be an incentive to a deeper study of the subject.

We describe separately the handling of wool and flax, from sheep and field to spun yarn and the completed article. There is a brief summary about the nettle as raw material. We have endeavoured to show how easy it is to acquire this knowledge and have given some idea of the requirements and economic aspects. The aim has been to take you step-by-step towards producing your own yarns for decorative and practical purposes. We wish you success!

Elisabeth Hoppe   Ragnar Edberg

Fig. I–1. The uneven result produced by the beginner can be taken advantage of as a decorative effect, and unspun wool may be inserted in a weave. Photo: Sven-Erik Sjostrom.

Fig. I–2. The sheep:
man's first domestic
animal, and source of
his wool. Photo:
Ragnar Edberg.

8

1. Wool

Wool can be described as that limited range of animal fibres suitable for weaving. The description both distinguishes the fibre from other animal hair (e.g. hairs of elephant tail, rope from pig's bristle, human hair) and places it as one of the most important natural materials for commerce.

There are many types of wool; the principal ones are as follows:

(1) *Sheep's wool* – from a large number of breeds; chiefly used for knitting and weaving.

(2) *Mohair wool* – from the Angora goat; noted for its lustre and decorative effect.

(3) *Cashmere wool* – from the Cashmere goat; for fabric and weaves.

(4) *Angora wool* – from the Angora rabbit; chiefly used for knitting.

(5) *Llama wool* – especially from the alpaca; for yarns and woven articles.

Some facts

● Wool is principally obtained by shearing or plucking a sheep or lamb, or pulling the wool from the skins of their carcasses. A more recent 'source' has been the re-cycling of wastage from textile processing.

● A single wool fibre varies considerably in diameter. It can be as fine as 10 microns (1 micron = 1/25,000 in.) and as thick as 50 microns; carpet wool is usually this thick and the fibres used in mattresses can be even thicker. Wool is therefore finer than flax and jute and thicker than cotton and silk.

● Fibre length varies according to diameter. Generally speaking fine wool is shorter than coarse; the reverse is true of cotton. Fine wool fibres can be as short as 1 in. (2.5 cm.) and coarse wool from a first clip can be as long as 12 in. (30 cm.).

● As well as having differences in fineness and length wool has important differences in physical form. Wool grows in locks or staples. In all the most attractive wool the fibres in any given staple are crimped, which means that they are curled, either in a regular wave or in a random, disorganized one; see fig. 1–2. The crimp (plus the ability of the fibres in a staple to retain their crimp) contributes to the bulkiness and warmth of fine wool. Conversely thin fabrics of parallel almost straight fibres are cool and compact.

*Fig. 1–1. Sheep
shearing is still often
done by hand. This
method causes far
less damage than
machine shearing. An
experienced sheep
shearer gets through
70–80 ewes per day.
Photo: Ragnar Edberg.*

● Wool differs in colour. Colours obviously vary according to breed of sheep so that there is black, brown or white wool. However there can also be considerable variations within one breed. This is due to a number of factors, including the extent of a sheep's belly that is urine stained and the discoloration that can be caused by particular pastures.

The amount of clean, as opposed to greasy or impure, wool on a sheep is known as the yield. The yield varies greatly according to climate, terrain and breed; for example some South African Merinos yield less than 45% good wool whereas English bred Lincolns can yield over 90% good wool. Listed below are some of the main causes of contamination:

(1) *Wool wax* – a lipid material, insoluble in water and secreted from the sebaceous glands.

(2) *Suint* – a water soluble component presumed secreted from the sweat gland.

(3) *Dirt* – sand, earth, ash and droppings; if pastures are windswept then collection of dirt tends to be worse; fleeces with a lot of wool wax or grease retain dirt more than purer ones.

(4) *Moisture* – fleece contains moisture; the moisture level will depend on atmospheric conditions.

(5) *Paint, tar, dip ointments and marking fluids* – in the past owners have used poor marking fluids when branding, and to kill insects and improve appearance have dipped sheep in watery fluids that have damaged the fleece. Recent developments in such fluids have reduced ruination.

(6) *Vegetable fault* – seeds and twigs become attached to the fleece while the sheep is feeding or lying down.

Quality

When discussing wool, the word 'quality' implies different things to different people. Apart from suggesting fitness for purpose, the word implies a statement of the type and origin of the raw wool. For example in England a good quality wool might mean to some that it is easily spun. Today each firm aims to produce a certain quality of yarn and is known accordingly.

Subjective judgments are important as the majority of woolmen like to judge quality according to how the wool

Fig. 1–2. The picture shows typical examples of wool. On the left, from the top: rya wool, tapestry wool, fine quality wool. On the right, three samples from the Swedish Päls breed and one from the Dala sheep. Notice the different crimps (or 'waves') in these staples of wool. Photo: Magnus Hoppe.

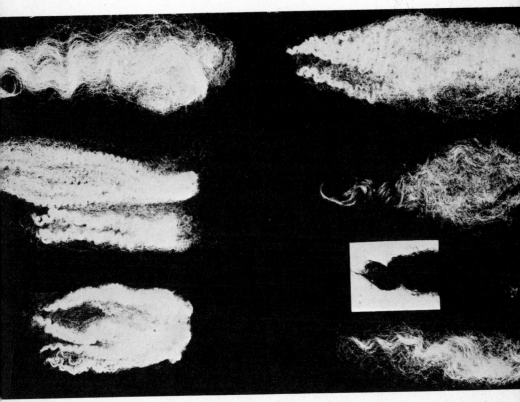

handles (especially important when considering spinnability) and how it looks. These judgments are made on the basis of sound knowledge about what governs quality. The factors include:

(1) *Variations in fibre fineness* – used a great deal in the U.S.A. and specified by the mean fibre diameter in a given staple of wool.

(2) *Crimp* – the association between fineness and crimp is only useful when sorting out the fleece or a group of fleeces that originate from the same place.

(3) *Length* – more useful as a subsidiary definition; length can influence both the spinning limit of wool (with fibre diameter) and the strength and extensibility of yarns (important when spinning wool near its breaking limit).

(4) *Other factors* – for high quality products wool should be of soft handling and should mill well. How far wool will extend before breaking (its plasticity) is important as wools in manufacture have to carry a constant and predetermined load of water. This plasticity is in turn associated with differences in fibre structures.

Grading

Subjective methods

Wool varies so much in its qualities that woolmen are convinced that fleeces from certain stations are more suitable for

Fig. 1–3. A ewe with pronounced shades of grey and with coarse kemp. During shearing hay and straw must be cleaned off the fleece to cut back the loss of wool as a result of vegetable matter. Photo: Ragnar Edberg.

their purposes than similar wool from other stations. It is also worth pointing out that the quality of wool can depend on what part of the sheep it was shorn from; see fig. 1–4. What is certain is the need for very sensitive ways of grading wool.

As we have seen woolmen like to judge wool subjectively by touch and sight. They are looking for particular qualities and there are several well known ways of testing:

(1) If you stroke wool gently then you can obtain an impression of smoothness or roughness (not to be confused with softness or hardness).

(2) If you hold a fabric firmly in the hand and squeeze you will get an idea of its resistance to compression.

(3) If you stroke and hold wool you will get an impression of its warmth.

There is a 'shorthand' for these impressions. The following table gives a guide to this 'shorthand' (it should be stressed that these terms are commonly used but not standard):

Terms for the handle of wool[1]

Term	Description	Opposite
Soft	This term may have two implications: (a) readily compressible, offering no resistance to the fingers (b) smooth – mohair and alpaca are often called smooth	(a) Hard (b) Harsh
Crisp	The term crisp may be regarded as denoting a property intermediate between soft and harsh. In the writer's opinion this term is more often applied in the scale of smoothness ((b) above) than in the scale of compressibility	
Lofty	Bulky, voluminous	Lean
Full	Bulky and resilient	Flat, cottony
Springy	Resilient, perhaps a harsher version of 'full'	Spongy
Warm	Fine, lofty wools feel warm. Locks of smooth, lean mohair feel cold	Cold

[1] Onions, W. J. *Wool, An Introduction to Its Properties, Varieties, Uses and Production.* Ernest Benn Ltd, London, 1972. An extremely useful survey of the entire field of wool technology.

Standard systems

Subjective judgments are not enough though, as they leave room for argument both between two people and whole countries. Several standard systems are in existence and as long as people agree which system to use then there is little room for dispute. We shall take a brief look at three:

(1) *The Blood System* – one of the oldest methods, originally derived from the fine wool Merino and Rambouïllet sheep. If one of these two was cross-bred then the resultant fibres were almost always coarser, or larger in cross-section diameter, than the pureblood. These wools were called one-half blood. Thus you can have a three-eighths blood, a quarter blood, etc.

(2) *The Numerical Count System* – derives from the blood system. The count refers to the number of 'hanks' of yarn, each 560 yd. long, that can be spun from 1 lb. of wool top. Thus a 50's would yield 28,000 yd. (560 yd. × 50) or 84,000 ft. of yarn. 80's denote a very fine yarn, 30's a very coarse one.

(3) *The Micron Count System* – the average diameter of wool fibre measured in microns (1 micron = 1/25,000 in.). This count is widely used today and is one of the most accurate.

Fig. 1–4. The best wool comes from the chest, sides and shoulders of the sheep (3). The quality of the wool on the back, neck and haunches is less good (1, 2, 4). The wool growing on the tail, legs and belly (5, 6, 7, 8) is often so heavily soiled that it has to be discarded. Photo: Ragnar Edberg.

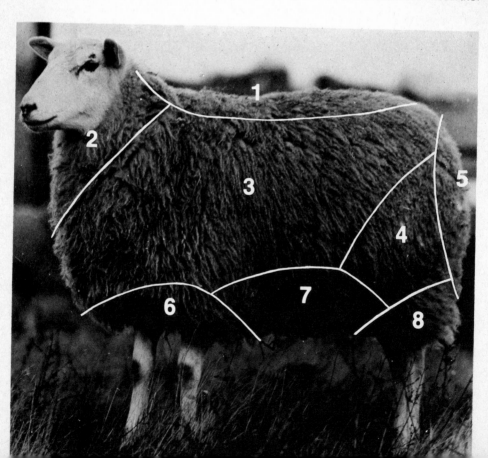

The wool textile industry

There are two different systems of producing wool yarns: woollen and worsted. The most important difference between the two is in the length of fibres they use, the worsted industry taking the long fibres and the woollen the shorter ones.

Woollen – the wool is scoured and carded into a web. The card web is then divided into slubbings, which are moderately stretched ('drafted') and spun.

Worsted – the wool is scoured and carded into a web. The web is delivered as a heavy sliver, is washed again, 'grilled' (drafted through sets of moving pins) and combed to remove the last remnants of vegetable matter, 'neps' (fibres in tight balls), and short fibre (sold to the woollen industry as 'noils'). The sliver of long, combed fibres is then grilled for a second time and wound into a big ball, called a 'top'.

The worsted industry divides here. Many firms (topmakers) simply produce tops and sell and export them to worsted spinners. Other firms make tops and do the spinning as well.

The wools processed in the woollen industry are referred to as clothing wools or carding wools; those of the worsted industry are known as combing wools.

2. Flax

Flax has always been an important natural material. For example, towards the end of the Middle Ages it became more and more usual among Northern European country folk to grow their own flax for domestic use in the household. As the centuries went by working with flax became increasingly important, until in some cases it was subsidized by the state, in the eighteenth and nineteenth centuries. There were many skilled spinners and weavers who received distinguished awards during this era, and the long preparation of the flax for spinning was done in groups to make the work lighter. When flax began to be imported cheaply from the Baltic States and elsewhere its cultivation declined. With the advent of machine-made cotton at the end of the nineteenth century, it disappeared altogether.

However, a few people here and there started growing flax again on a small scale and interest was aroused. In Sweden, institutes, housewives' associations and similar bodies now arrange so-called 'Linen Days' when the public can watch the preparation of flax as it used to be done. Some textile enthusiasts have also been tempted to try flax growing.

Anyone who wants to follow their example should make sure of getting the seed from Autumn Flax which produces a taller plant than the Spring Flax (the latter being grown for linseed oil), and to have the soil well manured and free from weeds. The seeds should be sown as close together as 5–6 in. (10–15 cm.) to prevent the plants spreading outwards and to encourage them to grow upwards.

Preparation

Flax is usually gathered when it turns golden and its seed capsules brown. Alternatively it can be harvested green when the fibre is thought to be at its best but the seeds are unripe. The linen will then be a delicate green at first, but the colour will disappear with washing and bleaching.

In the North of Sweden (our examples will come from Sweden as interest and expertise is high there) the saying goes that the flax must be harvested during 'the week before the frost'. The harvesting is done by pulling the stem so that the whole plant comes away. A bunch of plants is tidied

Fig. 2–1. Gathering
the flax. Photo:
Marianne Fischer.

and the root ends tapped against the ground to make them even at the bottom. The flax is divided into bundles and these are hung up to dry; see figs. 2–2 and 2–3.

Afterwards the seed capsules (the 'bolls') are combed off on a flax ripple. Incidentally the bolls are a delicacy for the birds and it is best not to crush them or some of the birds, like the robin with its thick beak, cannot get hold of the slippery seeds. For an example of a flax ripple (seed comb) see fig. 2–4.

Once the flax has been dried and the bolls removed, it can be left in a barn or other dry place until the preparation of the flax can be continued.

The next step in the preparation is the 'retting' (the partial rotting of the flax which frees the fibres from the stems).

In the North of Sweden water-retting was often used. The bundles of flax were lowered into gently flowing water, a lake or pond, where they were left to lie for a week or more. The time depended chiefly on the temperature of the water. A warning though – if flax is over-retted, the fibre becomes weak.

17

Fig. 2–2. The bundles of flax drying on a fence. Photo: Marianne Fischer.

Fig. 2–3. The root-ends face the same way and are made even. Photo: Marianne Fischer.

Fig. 2–4. Flax ripple from Knutby, Uppland, intended for two persons sitting astride the board facing each other, each alternately passing his bundle through the comb in the middle. Photo: Magnus Hoppe.

When the flax was thought to be sufficiently retted, it was taken up and rinsed in fresh water to stop any rotting. The flax was then carefully dried, first in the open-air and next in a drying room or sauna.

In other parts of Sweden land-retting was more common. Here the flax was spread out in a thin layer on sloping ground, on top of a stubble, or in a meadow. It was left there for three to five weeks (perhaps even longer depending on the temperature and moisture in the atmosphere). From time to time it was turned to prevent it from rotting on the side nearest the earth and from being scorched by the sun on the other side. Once the tops burst and the bast fibres curled then the retting process was complete. The flax then had to be dried. Once the flax had been thoroughly dried after the retting, it would keep for many years.

A method of retting, rarely used in Sweden but common in Holland and Belgium, was to use a retting pit, which was dug in ground containing blue clay. The flax was left to ret in it which gave the flax a blue sheen. The blue tint disappeared in the course of time in precisely the same way as the green tone of early-harvested flax mentioned on p. 16. Similarly, the silvery hue of fully ripened, well-retted flax faded when the linen had been washed a few times.

Fig. 2–5. When the flax is sufficiently retted the tops burst open and the bast fibres (or filaments) curl. Photo: Magnus Hoppe.

Although the natural tones of the flax generally disappear entirely when the linen is washed and bleached, the reddish hue does not vanish so easily. This is partly due to the quality of the soil and partly due to the flax being beaten down by wind and weather before harvesting (which also makes the flax rough and difficult to 'dress').

In order to be ready for the 'braking' the retted flax had to be dried until it was brittle. This could be done by making up a fire in a long trench and arranging the hanks on poles above it. The drying was done during the night before the braking was to start. The risk of fire was great, so a responsible older woman sat guard and turned the flax over at regular intervals.

In the braking process, which follows the retting and brittle-drying, the fibre and the woody part of the flax are separated by breaking or bruising the flax. This was done by various means: by pounding with a flax mallet; by working with a hand flax brake; by putting it through a braking mill with grooved rollers, see fig. 2–7.

Fig. 2–6. A flax mallet.

The warm flax stems were first put through the braking mill, if the village was lucky enough to possess one. If not, the coarse braking had to be done in one of the other ways mentioned above. Afterwards the flax was warmed up and the fine braking took place. The fine brake had an iron edge and was used for removing the woody parts. This was usually handled by the women as it was a more delicate operation than the coarse brake, which the men took charge of; see figs. 2–8 and 2–9.

The pole wedge was used like the fine brake, and the wedge was shod with iron.

'Scutching' removed the woody segments which remained after the braking. The flax was held over a scutching board (or scutching chair; see fig. 2–10) and the woody fibre, the scutch, was beaten out with the flax swingle (or scutching sword; see fig. 2–10) leaving the bast fibre. The scutch could be used for spinning a coarse thread, good for decorative textiles.

'Hackling' served to separate out the short fibres (which were spun into tow yarn) leaving only the long, glistening filaments. A hatchel was a board with long, sharp iron teeth; see fig. 2–12. Several hatchels were used successively, from coarse to fine.

Fig. 2–7. A braking mill. Photo: Magnus Hoppe.

21

Fig. 2–8. Coarse braking. Photo: Marianne Fischer.

Fig. 2–9. Fine braking. The flax is drawn over an iron edge underneath the middle shafts of a clamp. Photo: Magnus Hoppe.

22

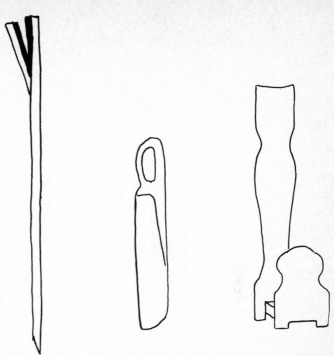

Fig. 2–10. From the left: a pole wedge, a scutching sword (swingle), a scutching chair.

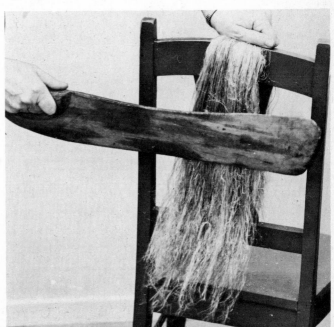

Fig. 2–11. Scutching can be done over the back of a chair. Photo: Magnus Hoppe.

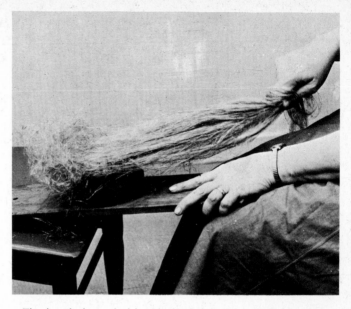

Fig. 2–12. Hackling. The hurds gather like a cloud at the top and remain there when the fibres are jerked free. Photo: Magnus Hoppe.

Fig. 2–13. Opposite. New hatchels in three sizes from coarse to fine being tried out at a 'flax preparation' day at the Runby Folksmuseum. Photo: Niklas Tyrefors.

The hatchel was held with the left hand and the flax by its roots in the right. First, the very coarse hurds were lightly drawn off for spinning into a coarse tow yarn or for mixing with the scutch. Again, the fibres were combed lightly over the top of the teeth; the hurds were gathered fluffily at the top of the flax and attached to the hatchel. Finally, the flax was drawn through in the whole of its length; this would produce the fine, soft fibres used in top quality linen. Sometimes a flax brush would be used, made of horse hair or pig's bristle, for brushing off the very last traces of hurd (or woody particles).

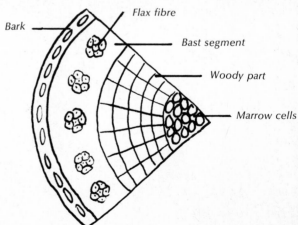

Fig. 2–14. Cross-section of the stem of flax. The various stages of preparation for the flax free its fibres for spinning.

24

3. Nettles

The fibres of the common stinging nettle provide excellent spinning material, and before the advent of cotton, nettle cloth was the finest weave made. The nettles are prepared in the same way as flax but are both harder to work and more sensitive.

Fig. 3–1. The common stinging nettle (Urtica dioeca) from which nettle cloth was made originally. Later the term nettle cloth came to mean very fine cotton cloth. Photo: Rune Kanger.

4. Carding

In order to be able to spin wool the fibres need to be parallel. The wool may be combed or carded, or spun straight from the tuft. Carding the wool is the most usual method. Combing is sometimes done in hand spinning when the fibres are too long to card.

Teasing

Good quality wool can very well be spun uncarded. In fact, in the countries where the spindle is still used for spinning, it is the usual way. A handful of wool is picked up with the cut ends uppermost; impurities are removed and the fibres are pulled apart gently between the hands. After this the fibres may be drawn and simultaneously twisted, which causes the barbs to hook on to each other, and the spinning can begin.

Carding

If, however, the wool is to be spun on a spinning wheel it is easier and quicker to spin if it has been carded beforehand. Well carded wool produces a yarn of good, even texture.

Only best quality wool should be used when carding. Tangled and soiled wool must have a preliminary carding with coarse spikes. However this is detrimental to the fibres.

Wool is best carded before washing. The wool should be kept at body temperature because it contains a lot of grease which makes it easy to card; if left to cool the grease congeals and makes the wool harsh and difficult to work. In the past, carding was often done with the wool spread out in front of a fire.

Take a few fibres, remove any vegetable matter, and pull them gently apart. Place the fibres on a carder, with the cut ends towards the handle and as much in line as possible; see fig. 4–1. The layer should not be too thick or it will be difficult to card the wool properly. Grip the carder with the left hand and place on the left knee with the handle away from the body. Draw the other carder lightly down against it with long movements towards the body; see fig. 4–2. The staples should now lie neatly.

When the wool has been carded through a few times it is transferred to the uppermost carder by drawing the latter

Fig. 4–1. The fibres are placed side by side on the carder with the cut ends towards the handle. Photo: Magnus Hoppe.

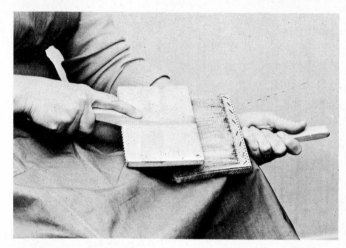

Fig. 4–2. Holding the carders. Photo: Magnus Hoppe.

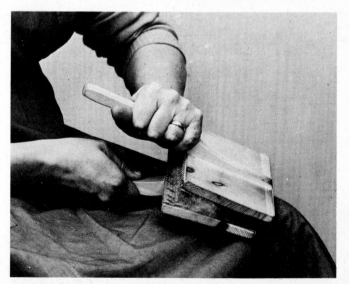

Fig. 4–3. For thorough carding, the wool must be turned at least twice, i.e. transferred to the other carder, then back again. Photo: Magnus Hoppe.

28

Fig. 4–4. Continue the carding until the wool is free of impurities and the fibres lie side by side. Photo: Magnus Hoppe.

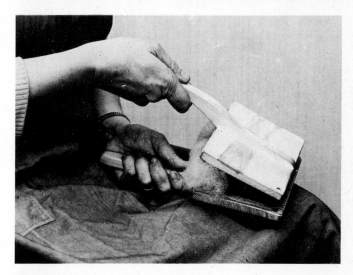

Fig. 4–5. The wool is rolled off the cards and is ready to spin. Photo: Magnus Hoppe.

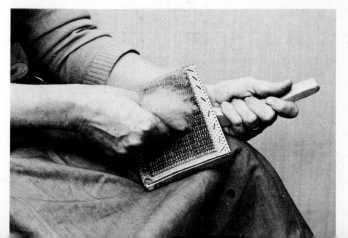

Fig. 4–6. The wool can be eased off as the picture shows . . . Photo: Magnus Hoppe.

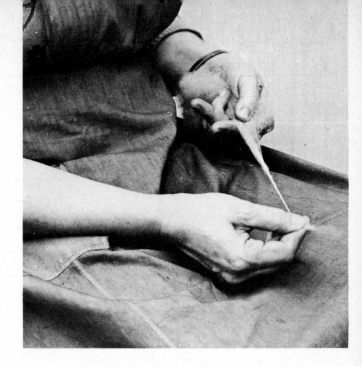

Fig. 4–7. . . . and spun
from the tuft. Photo:
Magnus Hoppe.

against the bottom one with the handles in the same direction; see fig. 4–3. Continue the carding and move the wool
to the opposite carder once more. The wool should not be
overcarded or it will tear.

When the wool appears free of foreign matter and the fibres
lie parallel, see fig. 4–4, the wool can be loosened from the
carders by passing one over the other with the handles in the
same direction; see fig. 4–5. This is done by forming the wool
into a roll with quick strokes and freeing it from the carder.
The fibres will be found to lie in coils forming a hollow tube.
The roll of wool is called a 'rolag'. For spinning, the fibres are
drawn from one end of the rolag, at the same time being
twisted. The fibres should be attached to the tie-in string,
which has already been attached to the spindle, and the spinning is done as described in Chapter 5.

Instead of shaping the wool into a rolag it can be eased off as
in figs. 4–6 and 4–7. The wool can be held as a tuft in the hand
when spinning; see fig. 6–10, p. 50.

Once you have carded the wool, it is ready for spinning.

5. Spinning

Why spin the yarn yourself?

In the old days, before machinery, it was very important to be able to spin a fine, even yarn. Nowadays, perfectly spun yarn of both wool and flax can be bought comparatively cheaply, so it does not pay to spin fine yarn by hand, even if the raw material costs nothing.

However, if the amount of wool at your disposal is small, or in varying qualities, it will be necessary to spin it at home because it is technically impossible to separate wools in machine spinning. Although it takes time to spin a fine yarn it can be done in odd moments, and practice will increase your

Fig. 5–1. A wrap, in lacy design, made of fine wool, spun on a spindle into a very thin yarn. Execution: Elisabeth Hoppe. Photo: Sven-Erik Sjostrom.

speed and skill. It is also a pleasant pastime to create the yarn which you will use to make something out of.

Recently decorative textiles with uneven surfaces and vivid colours have become popular. It is not always easy to buy yarns suited to this type of textile and they are also very costly. The yarns can be hand-spun quickly and easily, with the added advantage of only producing the exact amount needed, and with variations in colour and pattern according to choice. These yarns amply repay one for the work involved.

Begin with a stick

Spinning cannot be done without some tools. The basic implement is a round wooden stick about 1 in. in diameter and roughly 12 in. long. File away any roughness and round it at both ends. Cut a groove round the middle and fasten a string there of rug warp 12/6 or similar.

Flax is easier to spin than wool and does not require carding; the beginner finds it less difficult to handle with its long, sturdy fibres. For ready-to-spin flax see the list of suppliers on page 75. Alternatively you can practise on plumber's flax.

Start by drawing a few fibres from the bundle of flax, twisting slightly anti-clockwise; see fig. 5–2. Then attach the fibres to the tie-in string and make a half-stitch round one end of the stick (or spinning hook). Keeping the flax stretched with your left hand, roll the stick towards you with your right, thus causing the fibres to twist slightly (called roving or slubbing) as they are drawn from the bundle, and the yarn is formed; see fig. 5–3. Undo the half-hitch, wind the yarn on the middle of the stick, make another half-hitch round the end of the stick and start again from the beginning; see fig. 5–4.

It is a primitive method of spinning and a very slow one. However it is a good way to begin because it gives the learner time to get the feel of the process as the twisting and the stretching cause the barbs on the fibres to hook on to each other and form the yarn. After practice with the stick it is a good idea to go on to the spindle.

Opposite. Colour plate 1. Head-wear of felted wool embroidered with plant-dyed yarns, and a sock of handspun yarn from Icelandic wool. Design and execution: head-wear – Elisabeth Hoppe; sock – Inga-Lill Ingebo.
Colour plate 2. Sleeveless jumper of handspun yarn in various shades. The yarn was spun from white, grey and black wool and then dyed with indigo. Design and execution: Elisabeth Hoppe.
Colour plate 3. Knitted bag and mittens. The yarn was spun from coloured wool slivers. Design and execution: bag – Rita Lundberg; mittens – Birgitta Dahlberg. Photos: Sven-Erik Sjostrom.

1.   2.   3.

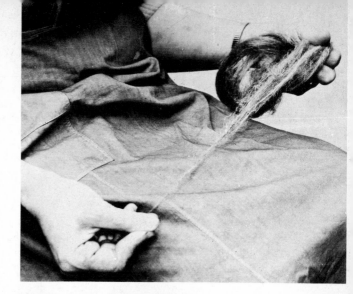

Fig. 5–2. A few fibres are drawn from the strick and are at the same time twisted slightly in an anti-clockwise direction (in the picture: towards the spinner). Photo: Sven-Erik Sjostrom.

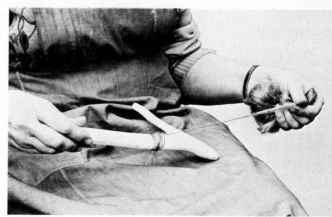

Fig. 5–3. The spinning hook (the roving hook) which is an ancient tool. Photo: Sven-Erik Sjostrom.

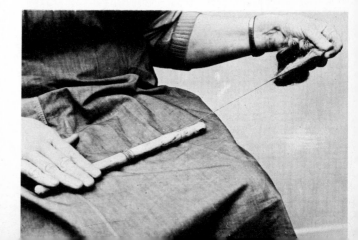

Fig. 5–4. The stick is rolled towards the spinner while the flax is kept extended with the other hand. Photo: Sven-Erik Sjostrom.

34

The spindle

The spindle consists of a thin, round piece of hardwood (about 12 in. long and ½ in. in diameter) and a whorl. The function of the whorl is to keep the spindle rotating. The precise weight of the whorl is important to ensure correct rotation, and should be enough to stretch the fibres without breaking them. On the other hand it must not be too light but well balanced in order to rotate smoothly without swaying. If the whorl is about 2½–3 in. above the bottom end, it allows the spindle to be held securely when winding and unwinding. Another type has the whorl at 2½–3 in. below the top, but this kind is usually more difficult for the beginner to manage. The tie-in string is attached above the middle of the spindle and may be passed through a notch or hook at the top. This helps to prevent any swaying which arrests the rotation and may break the thread. The pointed bottom end is the pivot which allows the rotation to continue, so long as the spindle remains at right angles to the firm object on which it rests.

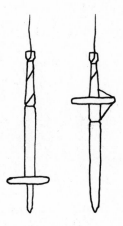

Fig. 5–5. Left: a down-weighted spindle. Right: an up-weighted spindle.

How to spin

Start with flax, or wool slivers (see p. 39) which are best used double as they are very brittle.

Draw some strands from the coil and twist them anticlockwise. Fasten the end to the tie-in string on the spindle and take the string to the top, meanwhile turning the spindle twice in a clockwise direction. Pass the string through the notch or hook at the top of the spindle.

Hold the yarn with the left hand, pinching it where it starts to twist so that the twist does not run towards the knop.

Hold the top of the spindle with the right hand, resting it on a chair or any object of convenient height. Start rotating it

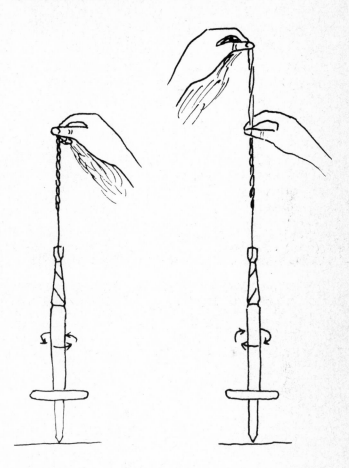

Fig. 5–6. Left. Hold the flax in a straight line above the rotating spindle. Right. As the flax is drawn from the knop, it is gripped higher up.

Opposite. Colour plate 4. Batik-dyed flax yarns. The coarser yarns are handspun and dyed without previous bleaching. The fine yarns are machine-spun and semi-bleached, then dyed.
Colour plate 5. Below right: table mat in traditional pattern from Dalana; warp and weft of indigo-dyed, home-grown and home-spun flax with pattern insertion of handspun nettle-hurds, dyed with greenwood. Below left: table mat. The weft consists of home-grown and home-spun flax in different natural colours. Idea and execution: Britta Stenberg-Tyrefors. Above right: a mat woven from home-grown and home-spun flax. Idea and execution: Inga-Lill Ingebo. Photos: Sven-Erik Sjostrom.

Fig. 5–7. Flax spinning on a spindle from strick on distaff. Photo: Sven-Erik Sjostrom.

Fig. 5–8. A long spindle.

Fig. 5–9. Opposite. Wool from five slivers in white and grey being spun together into shaded yarn on a long spindle. Photo: Sven-Erik Sjostrom.

in a clockwise direction, at the same time keeping the cord stretched upwards with the left hand in line with the spindle; see fig. 5–6, left.

As the spindle rotates, control the twist with the right hand below the left. Drawing more flax from the coil and keeping the twist from running out into the latter, move the left hand up the cord to the new position for controlling the twist. Wind the twisted yarn on to the spindle and continue as before.

The flax must run steadily from the knop through the hands and be kept fully extended between them, as well as between the left hand and the knop, with the twist not running back beyond the left hand; see fig. 5–6, right.

Once co-ordination between the hands has been achieved and the twists are regular and consistent, the spindle may be used hanging freely; see figs. 5–7 and 5–9. Spinning flax is made easier by having the fingers slightly wet.

When the spinning is finished, wind off the spun yarn.

You may also wish to experiment with uncarded wool.

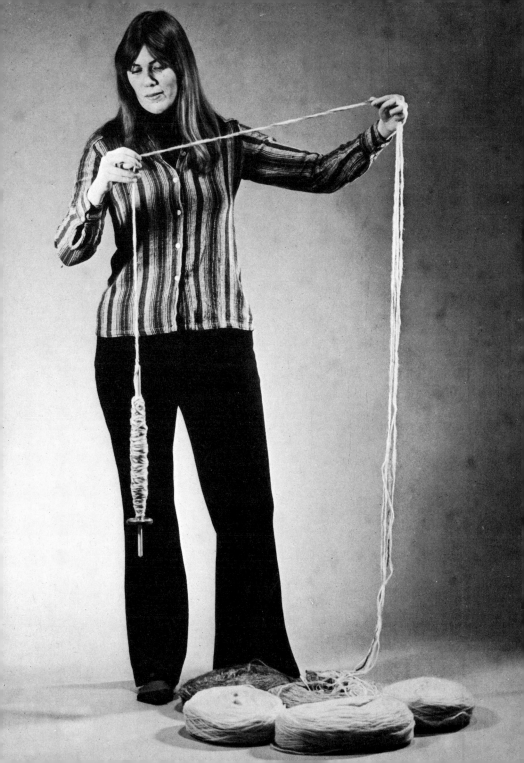

Fig. 5–10. Another way
of spinning: rotating
the long spindle by
rolling it up the thigh.
Photo: Sven-Erik
Sjostrom.

The long spindle

For spinning very coarse yarn, the spindle must be long,
preferably about 14 in., in order to accommodate the greater
bulk and to avoid frequent unwinding. Also, the whorl must
be heavier for the sake of the greater momentum required, as
well as to stretch the thick yarn. In ancient times whorls used
to be made of stone or baked clay. The spindle for coarse yarn
should have a fairly strong hook at the top.

It does not take long to learn how to spin on a long spindle.
It is especially useful for coarse, loose yarns which cannot be
spun on a spinning wheel as the yarns would catch on the
flyer.

Yarn may be spun together in four to six different colours or
white yarn can be spun together with different shades of grey
and perhaps a little black, and dyed afterwards (see Colour
plate 2).

Plying

Here the long spindle is also useful when two or more fine
yarns are to be twisted together. In this case the spindle is
rotated in the opposite direction to the one mentioned earlier.

From spindle to spinning wheel

The first spinning wheel was turned by hand. Then a treadle was added which left both hands free.

Fig. 5–11. Early design of spinning wheel. The wheel was turned by hand.

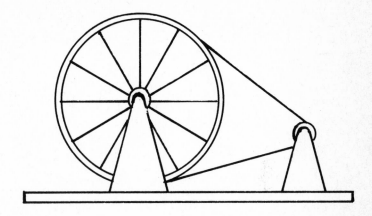

Fig. 5–12. Left. Type of tall spinning wheel with treadle. Right. Side view.

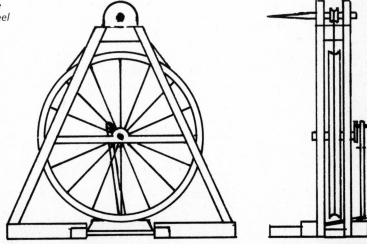

6. Spinning on a wheel

The spinning wheel

The spinning wheel was invented towards the end of the Middle Ages. It enables the spinning and the winding-on to be done simultaneously, and is a much quicker device than the spindle. However, the technique is more difficult to learn as several things have to be dealt with at the same time.

Fig. 6–1. New spinning wheel of traditional design. Courtesy of Glimakra Vävstolsfabrik.

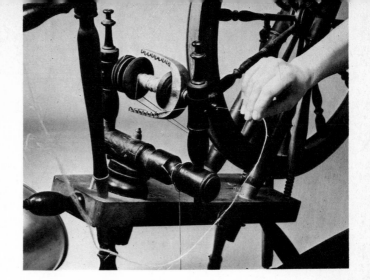

Fig. 6–2. Section of spinning wheel. The spun yarn runs through the 'eye' (or 'orifice'), over the guide hooks and is wound on to the bobbin. Photo: Sven-Erik Sjostrom.

The foot work must be nicely balanced by using a toe and heel motion. The pace must be slow enough to allow the wool or flax to be pulled-in and yet fast enough to keep the wheel revolving. If the wheel is not controlled it will reverse and break the yarn.

Since the amount of twist varies with different types of fabric, the twisting and pulling-in must be done to produce a yarn suitable for the purpose, whether soft with fewer twists, or firm and tightly twisted.

Fig. 6–1 shows a spinning wheel of traditional design. The three-legged, slightly inclined structure holds the wheel and the treadle, which are connected by a treadle rod. The wheel drives the flyer and the bobbin at the top end of the table by means of a double driving band.

Of the double driving band which passes twice round the wheel: one band drives the bobbin, the end of which is shaped like a whorl (the spindle whorl); the other band drives the flyer by means of a disc screwed on to the structure. The flyer is therefore fixed, while the bobbin is free to move by its own whorl.

The flyer has guide hooks which enable the yarn to be wound evenly on to the bobbin. As the fibres are twisted, they run through the spindle eye (technically known as the 'orifice', a hole in the part of the spindle facing the spinner), forming the yarn which runs through the guide hooks and is wound on to the bobbin; see fig. 6–2.

The tension between the wheel and the whorls is regulated by means of the tension screw in the higher end of the table.

How to spin

Tie a leader thread (tie-in string) to the bobbin. Take the thread over the guide hooks and out through the hole in the spindle, using a small hook. Begin as before, by drawing a few fibres from the tuft or rolag, and attach them to the leader thread.

Treadle the wheel in a clockwise direction to get the most common twist. It is important to make sure of always twisting in the same direction. Otherwise, when plying together several threads, trouble will arise through the different twisting and some will untwist.

Flax

Before starting to spin, you must make the flax into what is known as a 'strick' or 'line flax' for the distaff. This is done by taking a small bundle and folding it concertina-wise from the softest end, with the fibres parallel, then shaking it out and attaching it.

There are many different types of distaff. The spinning wheel shown on the cover has a short stick. Its forerunner was the long flax stick, which was used for spinning on a spindle. In figs. 6–3 and 6–4, the strick is attached to a flax comb by a long staff.

There are also distaff combs and distaff boards, as well as combinations of both.

Flax is best spun damp, which makes it smooth and lustrous. In primitive times, saliva was favoured as a means of wetting the flax, and resin would often be chewed to increase the saliva. Water can be used and should be lukewarm. If spun dry, the yarn may look smooth at first but later it becomes rough and bristly.

Opposite. Colour plate 6. Suit material with warp and weft of handspun, indigo-dyed yarn. (See p. 58.) Spun and dyed by Elisabeth Hoppe. Woven by Ruth Holm.
Colour plate 7. Two fabrics with a tie-dyed warp (see p. 64). The warp yarn in the brown twill material was dyed with lichen and indigo, the weft yarn with indigo. In order to make the pattern stand out, the material was woven using the warpsurface twill technique (see glossary). The material to the left is the front panel of a long skirt, and the pattern starts at the waist, follows the right side towards the hem and runs at right angles along it. The red material has both warp and weft dyed first with indigo, then with cochineal; the weft is slightly lighter and is woven as above. The pattern forms the border at the bottom of a dress. The dyeing and patterning were done by Elisabeth Hoppe, who also wove the red material. The brown material was woven by Ruth Holm. Photos: Sven-Erik Sjostrom.

6.

7.

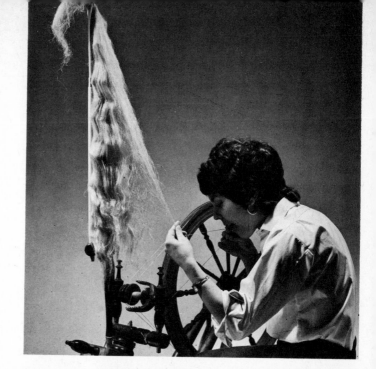

Figs. 6–3 and 6–4.
Wet-spinning of flax
can be done in
different ways. The
'strick' of flax in the
pictures is attached to
an unusual type of
flax comb. Photos:
Sven-Erik Sjostrom.

46

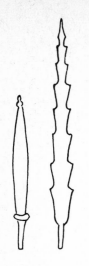

Fig. 6–5. Two types of distaff.

The hurds (or tow)

The hurds (also known as the tow) which are removed in the hackling can be spun into a good yarn, coarser or finer as desired, and depending on the quality of the hurds.

The hurds are placed in a holder which in the past could be cut from the tip of a pine tree. Fig. 6–7 shows a hurds holder of juniper.

Wool

Wool is not suspended but is held in the hand (usually in the left hand) with the right hand free for drawing out the fibres and preventing the twist from extending towards the rolag. Figs. 6–9 and 6–10 show two different methods of holding the wool.

With some practice it becomes possible to spin a fairly even yarn with a suitable twist.

By means of the screw, the relation is regulated between the twist and the winding-on.

Plying

Two or more threads may be plyed together by putting the actual bobbins on a bobbin holder, tying the ends of the leader string to an empty bobbin, and revolving the wheel in an anti-clockwise direction.

Fig. 6–6. Distaff of rectangular type (board), with combs for attaching the flax.

Fig. 6–7. Spinning from hurds. The holder is made of juniper. Photo: Sven-Erik Sjostrom.

8. 9. 10.

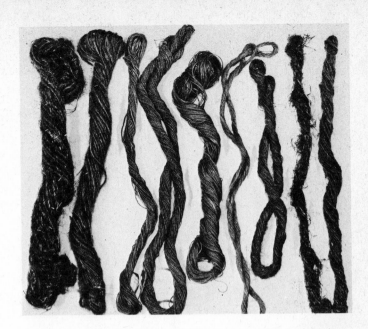

Fig. 6–8. Nine handspun yarns of different texture. From the left:
Yarn of coarse scutch; finer scutch; coarse hackle hurds (tip hurds);
finer hackle hurds. Coarse wet-spun flax yarn; fine wet-spun flax
yarn; dry-spun yarn of unheckled flax. The scutch from nettles
spun into coarse yarn; yarn of scutched but unheckled nettle
fibres. Photo: Magnus Hoppe.

Opposite. Colour plate 8. 'Sunflower seed'. Art-weave in
handspun, plant-dyed yarn. Idea and execution: Marianne Fischer.
Colour plate 9. Hand-woven dress material of plant-dyed wool.
Dyed with tansy plant. Varied mordanting accounts for the
different shades. Design and execution: Elisabeth Hoppe.
Colour plate 10. Circle of individually labelled, plant-dyed samples.
Britta Stenberg-Tyrefors. Photos: Sven-Erik Sjostrom.

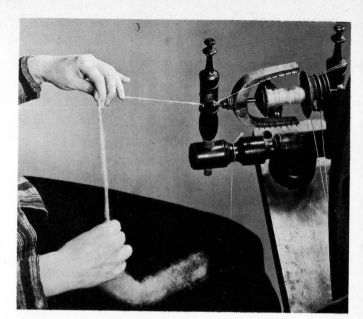

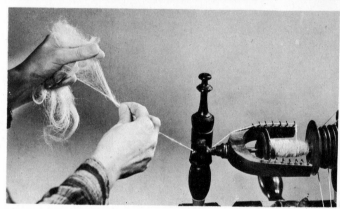

Figs. 6–9 and 6–10. Different ways of holding the wool for spinning. Photo: Sven-Erik Sjostrom.

7. Bleaching and dyeing flax

Bleaching

Linen is usually bleached after weaving, and more rarely in the yarn. When bleaching the yarn it is simmered in a weak solution of caustic soda, carefully rinsed, and hung out. The yarn must be turned from time to time so that it bleaches evenly.

Linen can also be bleached according to the following old recipe: To 16 oz. (454 g.) of yarn, take 1 oz. (28 g.) of soda dissolved in 450–630 fl. oz. (13–18 l.) of water. Simmer for an hour, then rinse very thoroughly. Whisk ½–⅔ oz. (14–20 g.) of chloride of lime into 450–630 fl. oz. (13–18 l.) of water and add 7–8 drops of nitric acid. Leave the yarn in the solution for eight hours, then rinse carefully.

If yarn, bleached in the above way, is to be dyed, let it simmer in plain water for an hour before dyeing, squeeze and put wet into the dye-bath.

On linen which is woven in a pattern with both bleached

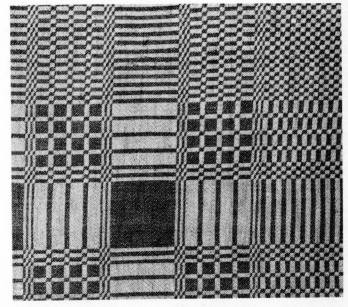

Fig. 7–1. Hand-woven table cloth from the 1930s. Warp of bleached cotton with weft of juniper-dyed flax. The flax was grown, dressed, spun and dyed by Linnéa Jansson, Danderyd, who also wove the cloth. Photo: Magnus Hoppe.

and unbleached sections, the pattern will get fainter with repeated washing, and finally disappear. This fading can be prevented by dyeing the unbleached yarn in water in which juniper has been boiled. This produces, approximately, the shade of unbleached linen. To obtain a purer grey, the same method may be used with spruce (*Picea abis*) and sulphate of iron.

Dyeing

Most plant dyes are unsuitable for the dyeing of flax. Exceptions are the dyes from bark, sticks, twigs and oak-apples, all of which give good results. The same applies to indigo which is a vat dye.

Vat dyes are insoluble in water and require the chemical process of oxygen reduction to make them soluble The dye-bath (vat) enables the textile fibre to absorb the dye. The oxidization which follows, through contact with the oxygen in the air and rinsing in water, returns the dye to its original condition of being insoluble in water. The colour pigment is then enclosed in the fibre which explains why the vat dyes are so resistant to washing and exposure to sunlight.

Vat dyes are best for the dyeing of flax (as well as cotton and rayon, all of which are cellulose fibres), because they are fast and will yield a wide range of shades.

When dyeing on a large scale the Swiss Ciba and Cibanon dyes may be used. They are not, however, obtainable in small quantities; ordinary batik dyes, also a vat dye, produce excellent results on both bleached and unbleached yarn.

8. Cleansing wool and woollen yarn

Before dyeing wool or woollen yarn, the grease and dirt must be carefully removed by washing, called scouring. There are various methods of scouring wool, but the material must always be treated gently, and the temperature of the water for washing and first rinsing should be 104°F. (40°C.). The subsequent rinsing can be done in slightly cooler water.

In the past, soft soap was considered ideal for washing, but nowadays different oils are used in its manufacture which cause the wool to felt too easily. (Soft soap is excellent, however, for felting wool and woollen yarn.)

Pure soap flakes with ammonia added to the water are best, and the scouring is done in two or three stages as follows: (skeins of wool should be tied loosely in a few places to avoid tangling)

I   420–470 fl. oz. (12–14 l.) warm water 104°F. (40°C.), 0·2 fl. oz. (5–6 ml.) 25%-ammonia.

   1 lb. (454 g.) wool yarn (or about 10 oz. (280 g.) wool sewn into a muslin bag). Leave the yarn in the water for 15–20 minutes (wool for a shorter time).

II   420–470 fl. oz. (12–14 l.) water, enough soap flakes to make a foam, 0·1 fl. oz. (2–3 ml.) 25%-ammonia.

   Squeeze the yarn gently in the soapy water. (The bag of wool should be moved gently to and fro and not squeezed, or the wool will felt.)

III 420–470 fl. oz. (12–14 l.) water, add soap flakes to make a foam.

   Wash as before but for a shorter period. Rinse: first at the same temperature, then in cooler water until clear.

9. Dyeing wool

It is very difficult to dye wool without it felting. When using vegetable dyes the temperature is usually maintained at 194°F. (90°C.) for about one hour. The wool yarn will stand up to these temperatures without harm, provided care is taken to avoid drastic changes in temperature.

Unspun wool is much more sensitive to heat and handling. One must therefore anticipate felting at a high temperature. Vat dyes, which require only a 104°F. (40°C.) temperature, are recommended.

For the following, batik dyes can be used. The foundation vat is prepared according to the instructions, except for caustic soda which is exchanged for 25%-ammonia in equal quantity. In addition, a solution of glue should be added to protect the fibre from undue effect of the alkali in the dye-bath (see recipe for indigo-dyeing, p. 59).

After dyeing, rinse in several waters, avoiding big changes in temperature. Add a little vinegar to the next rinsing water, and a drop or two of olive oil to the last rinse, especially if the wool is to be spun.

Then, spread out the wool to dry in gentle warmth, turning it over and fluffing it up at frequent intervals.

10. Synthetic yarn dyeing

In order to dye one's own yarn it is, of course, necessary to choose dyes intended specifically for wool yarn (or woollen materials). The dye must be perfectly fast and as resistant to fading as possible. It should also be easily obtainable in comparatively small quantities. Some synthetic dyes meet these requirements and are marketed in a sufficient number of colours, any of which can be mixed.

You can also try 'reactive' dyes, a fairly new group of dyestuffs which react chemically on the textile fibres: flax, cotton, rayon, wool and pure silk. The light- and washing-tolerance is above average. The dyeing is done at 77–122°F. (25–50°C.) for 20 minutes to 2 hours. No strong chemicals are required, only soda and cooking salt. These dyes are well worth trying.

11. Vegetable dyeing

EDITED BY GÖSTA SANDBERG

Gathering

Vegetable dyeing is surely the most interesting way to treat wool. If you collect the plant material yourself, the cost is very little and the joy of achievement all the greater.

Most plants can be used in a dried condition, so the dyeing

Fig. 11–1. Gathering plants for dyeing.

can be done at any time of the year. Present-day recipe books for dyeing with plants usually give the weight of the ingredients in the dehydrated state. It can be assumed that for a given weight, the dried article is usually twice as effective as the fresh. There are, however, plants which lose some dyeing power when dried, so the above estimate can only be given as a rough guide.

Other products, notably bark and roots, give better results after drying and storage. The root of bedstraw (*Galium boreale*) is an example. If the root is to be used fresh, it should be collected at the moment when the plant begins to flower and its strength is at a maximum. If the root is to be dried for later use, it should be dug up in late summer when the plant has finished flowering and the sap has returned to the root. After drying and storage, preferably for a year or more, it will give a stronger and deeper dye than the fresh root. The roots must be carefully washed before drying.

Bark, whether it is to be used dried or fresh, is collected in the spring when the sap begins to rise. It will then give a stronger dye and in addition is easier to strip from branches and twigs.

Green leaves and herbs should be collected at the moment when they are fully grown, but it is best to avoid gathering them during a prolonged period of drought. Plants which are to be dried should not be wet from rain or dew which can start mould or fermentation and destroy them. Plants which are to be used fresh must either be used immediately or kept in a cool place, perhaps in a jar of water.

A group of lichen called crottle which grows on stones and rocks should be collected after rain, otherwise it crumbles easily when scraped off the rock.

Mordanting

Most plants will yield dye substances, especially yellowish ones, but many of the colours fade very quickly, either partially or completely. It is therefore necessary to choose the best specimens and to cause the dye to 'bite' as durably as possible.

The only real vat dye in the plant world is indigo whose capacity to combine with textile fibres without previous mordanting has been mentioned in connection with the dyeing of flax (see p. 52). Other dyes which occur in the plant world are practically all 'adjective' dyes which require a mordant to reach the required standard of colour-permanence.

The yarn is usually mordanted before being dyed, but sometimes the mordant is mixed into the dye-bath, either at the beginning or sometimes only towards the end. By using different mordants different colours can be obtained from the same plant. Alum and tartar are common mordants, and can be used either separately or together.

The material used in the manufacture of the dye container may also affect the colour considerably (e.g. vessels of copper, iron and aluminium can change the colour) so it is best to use enamel or stainless steel at first to avoid surprises! With more experience though, even the substance of the vessel can be utilized to vary the colours.

Chromic acid darkens the dye and will, for example, make yellow dyestuffs brownish.

Tin crystals (Stannous chloride) are often used in conjunction with alum and tartar to obtain particularly vivid reds from cochineal, in which case the mordant is mixed in the dye-bath with the dye. Tin crystals must be used with great caution because they tend to make the yarn brittle.

Sulphates of iron and copper should generally be added to the dye-bath during the last fifteen minutes. Iron sulphate and copper sulphate are either used separately or together. Both have a marked darkening effect on certain dyes. The iron vitriol gives greyness, the copper vitriol brownness.

These mordants should also be used in small quantities because of their weakening effect on the yarn.

Unfortunately it is not possible to go very deeply into the mysteries of dyeing with plants. We have to content ourselves at present with general guidance and a few typical recipes. With care and patience, it is possible to experiment personally and learn in the process but without thorough knowledge valuable material could be wasted.

Dyeing with indigo (vat-dyeing)

Some readers may have experience of dyeing with batik dyes. This is one of the reasons why it seems advisable to start with indigo, which is prepared and used in a similar way.

A basic stock is prepared which can be kept for months in a vessel with a close-fitting lid. From the stock, baths of different strengths are made up: some, of course, dyeing blue; others are mixed for dyeing yellow to green, red to violet, and so on.

Basic stock

indigo	½ oz. (15 g.)
water, 122°F. (50°C.)	9 fl. oz. (250 ml.)
caustic soda (35% solution)[1]	0·6 fl. oz. (18 ml.)
sodium hydrosulphite[2]	just less than ½ oz. (15 g.)

Pound the indigo to a fine powder. Stir the powder with a few drops of methylated spirit in a bowl made of glass or stainless steel. Then add in the following order, stirring gently: the warm water, caustic soda and last of all the hydrosulphite which is sprinkled on top to avoid lumps. The basic stock is allowed to stand for an hour in a vessel with a close-fitting lid during which time it is kept at 122°F. (50°C.).

The basic stock which has now turned a yellowish brown, is then ready to add to the dye-bath. A sample is spread on a sheet of glass and should turn blue within a minute; if it does not, add more caustic soda and hydrosulphite.

Dyeing with indigo

The dye-bath can be made stronger or weaker depending on how much basic dye is added.

In order to protect the wool fibre against being too strongly affected by the alkali, a solution of glue is added, ⅓ oz. (10 g.) of glue granules dissolved in 3·5 fl. oz. (100 ml.) water. The solution of glue soon deteriorates and has to be made up fresh each time.

The glue solution and chemicals are proportional to the quantity of basic stock. The amount of water can be greater or less without appreciably affecting the strength of the dye. The yarn absorbs the amount of dye which is in the bath.

Below are two different methods for dyeing blue with indigo.

INDIGO I

water, 122°F. (50°C.)	420 fl. oz (12 l.)
glue solution	0·9 fl. oz. (25 ml.)
ammonia (25%)	0·4 fl. oz. (13 ml.)
sodium hydrosulphite	⅙ oz. (5 g.)
stock	0·5 fl. oz. (15 ml.)

---

[1] 35% solution = just over 1 oz. (30 g.) caustic soda to 0·35 fl. oz. (10 ml.) water.
[2] sodium hydrosulphite must be stored in an airtight container in a dry place.

Fig. 11–2. In tie-dyeing, sections of the yarn are tied round or put in plastic bags.

Fig. 11–3. The yarn is turned over from time to time so that it dries evenly.

The water, which must be 122°F. (50°C.) and maintained at this temperature throughout, is poured into a stainless steel or enamel vessel. Add chemicals and glue solution. Stir the stock gently before measuring it in a graduated glass and add it to

the dye-bath, which should turn a clear yellowish green – possibly with dark-blue bubbles. If the bath is blue or curdles, further chemicals must be added to reduce the oxygen which has, for some reason, entered the bath.

We shall now use this dye-bath for tie-dyeing. A batch of about 16 oz. (454 g.) yarn is dipped in water at 104°F. (40°C.), squeezed, and plastic bags are tied round each end; see fig. 11–2. The yarn is then immersed in the dye-bath and moved gently to and fro for 10 minutes. The yarn is then lifted out and allowed to oxidize in the air for 10 minutes.

When the oxidization has been completed after the last dyeing, it is possible to decide whether or not the result is satisfactory. If not, the batch can be re-dyed, with or without tying.

This expedient is particularly suitable for superimposing other colours, like yellow and red.

The yarn is washed and rinsed very carefully, first in lukewarm, then in slightly cooler water. Add a little (white) vinegar to make the last water acid. Dry the yarn in the open, in the shade, arranged on rods. The yarn must be turned from time to time, so that it dries evenly; see fig. 11–3.

INDIGO II (traditional recipe)

water, 122°F. (50°C.)	210 fl. oz. (6 l.)
glue solution	1·8 fl. oz. (50 ml.)
ammonia (25%)	0·9 fl. oz. (25 ml.)
sodium hydrosulphite	⅓ oz. (10 g.)
stock	1 fl. oz. (30 ml.)

The water, which is to be kept at a constant temperature throughout the process, is poured into a stainless steel or enamelled vessel.

The chemicals are added in the above order, and last of all the foundation dye after gently stirring. The dye-bath must be a clear yellowish green. 4 oz. (113 g.) yarn is moistened in 104°F. (40°C.) water, squeezed and placed in the dye-bath where it is moved gently for 30 minutes. The yarn is lifted out, allowed to oxidize for a while and put in 104°F. (40°C.) rinsing water. The yarn turns a very strong shade of blue.

The dye-bath is strengthened to receive the next bath by adding 0·4 fl. oz. (12 ml.) ammonia and sodium hydrosulphite and some glue solution. The same amount of fresh yarn is moistened, dyed in the same way and placed in rinsing water.

The procedure can be repeated so long as the bath gives colour – usually about four times. Weak dye makes for poor resistance to light and washing. A variety of blue shades may be obtained in this way, from dark to light blue.

Yarns must be washed and rinsed very carefully. Add vinegar to the last rinsing water.

'Stuffing' (mixing mordant and dyestuff)

Tansy (Tanacetum vulgare)

Below are some recipes for dye which can be extracted from the leaves of the tansy (Tanacetum plant), using various mordants. The resulting yarn has been used for a striped warp as well as a uniform yellow weft; see Colour plate 9, opposite p. 49. (For weaving instructions see: Hoppe, E., Ostlund, E., Melen, L., *Free Weaving on frame and loom*, Van Nostrand Reinhold, London and New York, 1974.)

Fig. 11–4. If the leaves are put in layers among the yarn, a stronger colour is obtained but the dyeing is liable to be patchy.

Most of the yarn is mordanted in alum which enhances the natural colour of the dye. For every 3 oz. (100 g.) of yarn take 78·8 fl. oz. (2·2 l.) of water and ⅔ oz. (18·8 g.) of alum. Soak the yarn in water at 104°F. (40°C.), squeeze and place in the warm mordant, which is then brought up to 194°F. (90°C.) and is kept at this temperature for an hour.

A small part of the yarn will form yellowish brown stripes in the warp and is therefore mordanted with bichromate of potash. For every 4 oz. (113 g.) of yarn take 78·8 fl. oz. (2·2 l.) of water and ⅑ oz. (3 g.) of bichromate of potash. Proceed in the same way as for alum mordanting.

The brightest yellow colour comes from fresh leaves which have been picked immediately before flowering. The leaves are chopped up and put in layers between all the previously mordanted yarn. If the yarn has been dried after mordanting, it must first be immersed in warm water and squeezed. Use plenty of leaves and make sure that they amply cover the bottom and sides of the vessel. The water must completely cover the yarn and all the leaves. Heat the bath to 194°F. (90°C.) (and maintain at this temperature for 30 minutes), remove from heat and let it stand overnight.

On the following day, remove the yarn, squeeze it and shake out the leaves. Strain the dye-bath and add $\frac{1}{18}$oz.(1·6 g.) of potash (potassium carbonate) per 4 oz. (113 g.) of yarn. The yarn, which was mordanted with bichromate and is now dyed yellowish brown, is separated out and placed in lukewarm rinsing water. The rest of the yarn, which is now yellow, is put into the dye-bath, heated to 194°F. (90°C.) and kept at this temperature for 30 minutes. Lift the yarn and separate out all that portion which is required to be a bright yellow, and place it in lukewarm rinsing water.

The yarn which is to form the yellowish green and the greyish green stripes in the warp must now be given further treatment. Divide the dye between two vessels. To one end of them add about $\frac{1}{9}$oz.(3 g.) of copper sulphate per 4 oz. (113 g.) of yarn, and to the other the same amount of iron sulphate. Put the hanks into their respective baths and heat once more to 194°F. (90°C.). Maintain this temperature for 15 minutes. The bath containing copper sulphate will make the yarn a yellowish green, that with iron sulphate makes the yarn darker and more of a greyish green. The yarns are washed and rinsed very carefully. The yarn treated with iron sulphate must have some vinegar in the last rinsing water. Dry without further rinsing, to retain the acid.

The weft yarn (alum mordanted) is dyed with a decoction of the entire dry plant. Reckon ¼ lb. (113 g.) of dried tansy and 80–160 fl. oz. (2·3–4·5 l.) of water to each 4 oz. (113 g.) of yarn. Boil the 'soup' for one hour, let it cool off a little and replenish the water which has evaporated. Steep the yarn in water at 104°F. (40°C.), squeeze it and place it in the bath, stirring gently with a stick meanwhile to ensure even dyeing. Heat the bath to 104°F. (90°C.) and maintain this temperature for one hour, then wash and rinse well.

In order to obtain strong green colours one can super-impose indigo on tansy-yellow, or put indigo-dyed yarn in the tansy-bath.

Other easily obtainable plants which give a good yellow colour include birch leaves (*Betula alba*), lady's-mantle (*Alchemilla vulgaris*), cow parsley (*Anthriscus silvestris*), ling (*Calluna vulgaris*) and barberry (*Berberis vulgaris*).

Try different methods and mordants in accordance with recipes given above.

Lichen and indigo – patterned warp

The lichens have been well known through the ages as excellent plants for dyeing. One of the crottles (*Parmelia saxatilis*) is one of the best known of the lichen dyes. It gives various shades of brown, depending on the method and the mordant used. Mordanting is not always necessary. Below is a recipe for a lichen dye.

You can achieve a patterned warp in the same way that marl yarn with a flame effect can be obtained by tying the skein in a few places. This technique is thought to have originated in Indonesia and is called *Ikat*. The procedure is as follows:

(1) Stretch the warp between two rods so that the patterning may be planned.

(2) Tie with strings of strips of material those sections which have to be protected from the brown dye; see fig. 11–5.

(3) Put ties loosely round the whole warp in several places.

(4) Make sure shed is kept in order during dyeing.

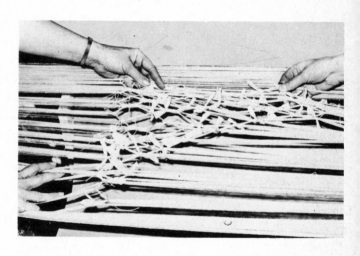

Fig. 11–5. Warp tied with tapes and strings to isolate sections in order to form pattern; (see Colour plate 7, opposite p. 44).

REDDISH BROWN WITH CROTTLE (*Parmelia saxatilis*)
Allow 14 oz. (400 g.) dried lichen per 4 oz. (113 g.) of yarn.

The yarn should not be pre-mordanted but wetted and squeezed out. The lichen is divided up into small pieces and put in layers with the wet yarn into a stainless steel pot. The thicker the layers of lichen, the darker the yarn.

Pour in cold water and let it stand overnight. The water should cover the lichen and yarn.

Heat to 194°F. (90°C.) and maintain this temperature for 2–4 hours, stirring now and then. The yarn can well be left to cool in the dye-bath. When the yarn is taken out it will be full of bits of lichen. These must be shaken off and rinsed out. Rinse the yarn carefully.

The ties for the pattern are removed, revealing the undyed sections. The warp is rinsed again before being dyed in indigo. The indigo makes the reddish dye darker and less red; sections not previously dyed will, of course, become blue.

The warp is dyed in a fairly weak indigo bath. For recipe, see Indigo I, page 59.

Dye for 10 minutes, oxidize for 10 minutes. For a stronger shade, repeat the process. Wash and rinse according to the recipe.

Most of the moisture can be pressed out between turkish towelling. Then dry the warp spread out between the rods in the same way as for tie-dye.

To make the warp pattern stand out as much as possible, weave in a warpsurface twill; see glossary. For the weft, a medium light blue or perhaps brown yarn can be chosen.

As we mentioned earlier, the lichens will provide many different shades of brown.

It is possible to dye in a strained decoction of lichen. The colour is fainter but it is easier to get the dye to bite evenly.

Pre-mordanting can be done with alum and cream of tartar. Also iron or copper sulphate can be added towards the end of the dyeing.

The proportion of lichen to yarn may also be varied.

Cochineal

Cochineal is not a vegetable dye but comes from an insect reared on some species of cacti. The fertilized females are gathered and dried. Cochineal gives a strong red colour. It is used, for instance, in the manufacture of lip-stick.

Below are the recipes for two series of red dye extracted from cochineal. The difference between them arises from the different ways of mordanting.

COCHINEAL I

Cochineal I gives a range of bright red dyes and the same dye-bath can be used several times. The yarn should not be pre-mordanted.

4 oz. (113 g.) of yarn will require:

cochineal	½ oz. (14 g.)
cream of tartar	½ oz. (14 g.)
tin chloride crystals	⅛ oz. (3 g.)
nitric acid	0·2 fl. oz. (6 ml.)
water	158 fl. oz. (4·5 l.)

Fig. 11–6. The yarn is drawn over rods to make the dye act as evenly as possible.

On the day before, powder the cochineal in a mortar and put it to soak overnight.

Then, bring the water to the boil, add the cochineal and the tartar, which must be completely dissolved. Leave to boil for 10 minutes, then skim.

Add the tin crystals and the hydrochloric acid, stir and let the bath cool off for a little while.

Damp the yarn in warm water, squeeze it and put it into the dye-bath, drawing it over rods for the first 10 minutes to make the dye act as evenly as possible. Dye the yarn for 60–90 minutes at 194°F. (90°C.) and wash and rinse in the usual manner. Add vinegar to the last water.

Continue using the bath for after-dyeing while the dyestuff still bites, adding half the original amount of tartar, tin crystals and acid each time.

Beautiful violet shades can be obtained in the above dye-bath on yarn previously coloured by indigo.

COCHINEAL II

Cochineal II gives a series of red dyes with a tendency towards blue. The yarn must be pre-mordanted with alum and tartar.

For the mordanting of 4 oz. (113 g.) of yarn, the following are needed:

alum	⅔ oz. (20 g.)
cream of tartar	⅓ oz. (10 g.)
water	175 fl. oz. (5 l.)

Mordant for 60–90 minutes at 194°F. (90°C.).

For the dyeing of 4 oz. (113 g.) of yarn the following are needed:

cochineal	⅔ oz. (20 g.)
water	175 fl. oz. (5 l.)

Powder the cochineal in a mortar and put it to soak the day before. Bring water to the boil, add the cochineal, allow to boil for 10–15 minutes and remove scum.

Let the bath cool a little. Damp the yarn in warm water, squeeze and place it in the bath where it is drawn over rods for the first 10 minutes and then dyed for 60 minutes at 194°F. (90°C.). Wash the yarn and rinse it carefully but without added vinegar.

The bath can be used for after-dyeing; the yarn must be mordanted in the same way as before, but the bath is not strengthened with additional chemicals.

To obtain violet shades, add indigo.

Yellowish red dyes

Yellowish red or brownish red dyes can be made from the root of the madder, a plant growing wild in the Mediterranean countries. It can be purchased dried and ground. Similar results can be obtained from northern bedstraw (*Galium boreale*) which is of the same family as madder. It is to be found on sandy soils, especially Northern England, Scotland and Ireland. Use four times as much bedstraw as madder.

The roots must be thoroughly cleaned and can be used fresh or dried.

YELLOW RED OR BROWNISH RECIPE

The yarn is mordanted in a bath of:

alum	⅔ oz. (20 g.)
cream of tartar	⅓ oz. (10 g.)
water	175 fl. oz. (5 l.)

to 4 oz. (113 g.) yarn. Mordant for 60 minutes at 194°F. (90°C.). For this amount of yarn you will need, depending on the strength of colour required:

root of bedstraw	4–16 oz. (113–454 g.)
water	175 fl. oz. (5 l.)

Fig. 11–7. The last rinse can be done in the lake.

Chop the roots into pieces and leave to soak overnight. Heat the bath to 158°F. (70°C.) without previous straining.

The mordanted yarn is steeped in 104°F. (40°C.) water (lukewarm); squeeze and put into dye-bath for 60 minutes. During the first ten minutes draw it over rods to ensure even action of the dye. For browner shades raise the temperature to 194°F. (90°C.), then wash and rinse yarn.

Zinnia flowers and dahlia flowers give several different yellowish red dyes.

It is possible to experiment with different kinds of mordant such as alum, tartar or both together, as well as tin crystals which give a more reddish tone.

12. Summary of preparation and uses of wool and flax

Wool is made into yarn

Wool can be spun uncarded, washed as yarn or fabric.
Wool is carded and spun, washed as yarn or fabric.
Wool is carded and spun, washed and dyed as yarn or fabric.
Wool is carded, different natural colours separately, spun together and washed. The yarn will be in shades of grey.
Wool is carded, different natural colours separately, spun together, washed and dyed. Yarn of mixed colours.
Wool is carded, different natural colours separately, spun together with dyed wool, washed. Yarn of mixed colours.

Other ways of using wool

The wool is washed, divided into tufts for art weaving.
The wool is washed and carded for art weaving.
The wool is washed and dyed, divided into tufts for art weaving.
The wool is washed, dyed and carded for art weaving.

Felting: fine quality wool is carded, placed in two or more layers one over the other but with the fibres crossing. Work together by damping with lukewarm water with soft soap in it, and rub with fingertips partly shaping the wool. Continue working the wool on a wash board. Rinse in cold water.

Flax: preparation and result

Retting	Braking	Scutching	Hackling	Spinning	Yarn
×	×	×	×	×	Flax yarn
			by-products	×	Tow- or hurd-yarn
×	×	×		×	Coarse yarn with wood segments
		by-product		×	Scutch yarn

Dyeing chart

Recommended dye substances:

Type of fibres		Mordant dyes	Vat dyes	Reactive dyes	Synthetic dyes
		Plant dyes in general	Batik-dyes Indigo	Zenit Silk-batik dyes	
Protein fibres	Wool Pure silk	×	×	× ×	× ×
Cellulose fibres	Flax Cotton Rayon	Best with twigs, bark, branches	× × ×	× × ×	
Polyamide fibres	Nylon Perlon etc.				× ×

Glossary

Adjective dyes: dyes requiring a mordant.

Batik dyes: a group of chemical dyes.

Bleaching: exposing textile fabrics to sunlight or chemicals for whitening.

Bobbin: the part of the spinning wheel on which the spun yarn is wound.

Bolls: seed pods of flax or cotton.

Braking: breaking up of woody stem in flax.

Card yarn: spun from wool prepared by carding.

Carders: hand implements used for carding.

Carding: cleaning, disentangling and ordering wool, preparatory to spinning.

Cochineal: a red dyestuff consisting of the dried bodies of females of the cochineal insect.

Comb yarn: also called worsted and prepared by separating the long fibres from short by combing.

Crottle: a group of lichens used in vegetable dyeing.

Distaff: a staff for holding a bunch of flax during spinning.

Double driving-band: a continuous length of band passed round the rim of the spinning wheel, over the whorl, again round the wheel then over the bobbin.

Dye: substance – vegetable matter or chemical – giving colour to fibre or fabric.

Dyeing: the work involved in adding colour to fibre or fabric.

Dye-bath: the ready-made solution for dipping fibre or fabric.

Fading: losing freshness of colour.

Fast: (of dyes) resistant when exposed to sunlight or washing.

Felting: the working together of fine quality wool. The wool is carded, placed in two or more layers one over the other but with the fibres crossing. Work together by damping with lukewarm water with soft soap in it and rub with fingertips, partly shaping the wool. Continue working the wool on a wash board. Rinse in cold water.

Flax: plant of the family Linum, fibre from which is used in linen production.

Flyer: the part of the wheel which twists the yarn while spinning.

Guide hooks: small hooks attached to the flyer; the purpose being to distribute evenly the spun yarn on the bobbin.

Hackling: clearing out short fibres from flax.

Hank: a coiled bundle of yarn.

Hurds: waste material from flax fibres.

Leader thread: a 12–18 in. long thread tied to bobbin on

spinning wheel to 'lead on' the yarn at the start of spinning.
Lichen: primitive plants growing on rocks, old wood etc.
Source of many vegetable dyes.
Marl yarn: yarn of mixed colours.
Mordanting: preparation of textile fibres to enable the dye to
'bite'.
Oxidization: in dyeing with indigo– exposing the dyed mater-
ial to the air.
Plying: twisting two or more threads together.
Reactive dyes: dyes reacting chemically on the fibre.
Retting: soaking flax in order to loosen the woody part.
Rolag: wool carded, ready to spin.
Roving or slubbing: drawing out and twisting fibres slightly.
Scouring: washing of textile fibres.
Scutching: removing woody segments from flax fibre.
Shearing: cutting the wool from the sheep.
Skein: small coil of yarn.
Spinning: turning fibre into a continuous thread.
Spindle: usually a stick fitted with a disc used for spinning.
Spinning wheel: wooden implement used in the home for
spinning.

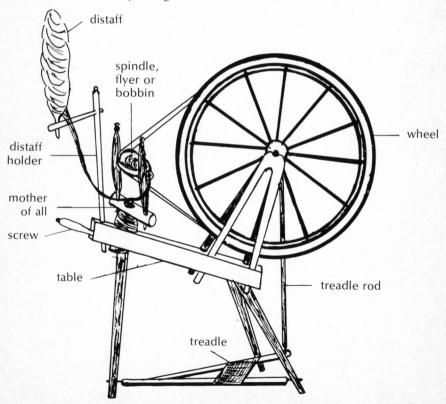

Strick: a bundle of flax fibres.
Stuffing: mixing the mordant in the dye-bath.
Tansy: dye plant (*Tanacetum vulgare*).
Tensions screw: part of spinning wheel, regulating the tension between wheel, whorl and bobbin.
Tie-dye: a dyeing technique in which fabric or yarn are tied with tape or strings to isolate parts in order to resist the dye.
Treadle: a footboard which operates the spinning wheel.
Treadle Rod (Footman): rod connecting footboard to wheel.
Tuft: bunch of fibre.
Twill weave: weaving technique on four shafts.
Twisting and Pulling: the process of spinning the yarn.
Vat dyes: organic dyes insoluble in water, e.g. indigo.
Vegetable dyes: all dyes from plants.
Warp: the yarn extended lengthwise on the loom.
Warpsurface Twill Technique: a weaving technique where the warp threads dominate the surface of the cloth.
Weft: the yarn going crosswise through the warp.
Weft yarns: yarns specially used for weft with a slightly loose twist.
Whorl: a pulley drawing the flyer on a spinning wheel.
Wool: animal hairs used in textile production.
Yarn: a continuous strand made from textile fibre.

Further reading

Books of related interest from Van Nostrand Reinhold

ON WOOL

Bowen, G. *Wool Away, The Art and Technique of Shearing*. New York and London 1974.
208 pp. 20 line drawings, 61 halftones. 8½ × 5⅜.

ON SPINNING AND DYEING

Castino, R. *Spinning and Dyeing the Natural Way*. New York and London (Evans Brothers), 1974.
100 pp. 126 photos. 4 pp. in colour. 9¼ × 8¼.

ON DYEING

Robertson, S. *Dyes from Plants*. New York and London, 1974.
128 pp. 84 illus. 8 pp. in colour. 9¼ × 8¼.

Nea, S. *Tie-dye*. New York and London, 1971.
108 pp. 100 illus. including 60 design diagrams. 12 pp. in colour. 8 × 6.

Nea, S. *Batik*. New York and London, 1971
100 pp. 100 illus. 4 pp. in colour. 8 × 6.

Krevitsky, N. *Batik: Art and Craft*. (Paperback edition) New York and London, 1973.
92 pp. 124 illus. 6 pp. in colour. 8 × 8.

ON WEAVING

Kroncke, G. *Simple Weaving*. New York and London, 1973.
96 pp. 122 illus. 40 halftones. 72 line diagrams. 8 × 6.

Hoppe, E., Ostlund, E., Melen, L. *Free Weaving on Frame and Loom*. New York and London, 1974.
108 pp. 63 halftones. 71 line drawings. 12 pp. in colour.

Regensteiner, E. *The Art of Weaving*. New York and London (Studio Vista), 1970
184 pp. 244 halftones. 70 line drawings. 122 pp. in colour.

Suppliers

AUSTRALIA

Charles D. Bailey, 15 Dutton Street, New South Wales. Dyestuffs, fibres for spinning (fleece, cotton, silk, mohair).

UNITED STATES

Christopher Farm, R.F.D. No. 2, Richmond, Maine 04357. Quality yarn from their 350 Corriedale, Montdale and Columbia sheep. Their yarn is mill-spun but nice.

City Chemical Company, 132 West 22 Street, New York, N.Y. Mordants and other chemicals.

Clemes & Clemes, 665 San Pablo Avenue, Pinole, California. Spinning wheels, supplies for spinning such as spindles, distaffs, cards, etc.

Earth Guild, Inc., 149 Putnam Avenue, Cambridge, Mass. Dyestuffs, mordants, spinning wheels; and fibres (wool, alpaca, and various others).

R. A. Meisterheim, R.R. 6, Box 242, Dowagiac, Michigan. Spinning wheels sold, repaired and restored.

Natural Science Industries, Ltd., 51–17 Rockaway Beach Blvd., Far Rockaway, New York 11691. 'Silk factory', kit for raising silk worms.

The Niddy-Noddy, Croton-on-Hudson, N.Y. Unusual yarns, weaving and spinning supplies.

Sargent-Welch Scientific Company, 7300 North Linder, Skokie, Illinois 60076. Biological supplies, including 'Silk garden' kit for raising silk worms.

Marguerite Shimmina, 2470 Queensbury Road, Pasadena, Calif. Silkworm eggs. Write first for description of supplies.

Paula Simmons, Suquamish, Washington. Handspun yarns and items woven of handspun yarn.

The Spinster, 34 Hamilton Avenue, Sloatsburg, N.Y. 10974. Unique handspun yarns to order, fibres (Corriedale, Cheviot, Dorset, and Karakul fleeces, silk, alpaca, mohair, camel's hair, cashmere, cotton, flax).

Yarn primitives, P.O. Box 1013, Weston, Connecticut 06880. Imported handspun yarns, including alpaca, goat hair, cotton, and others.

CANADA

Handcraft House, 56 Esplanade, North Vancouver, British Columbia.

Nilus LeClerc, Inc., L'Islet, Quebec. Looms and a complete selection of weaving supplies.

Village Weaver, 551 Church Street, Toronto, Ontario.

Mrs E. Blackburn, R.R. No. 2, Caledon East, Ontario.

UNITED KINGDOM

Spinning and weaving equipment:

Dryad, Northgates, Leicester.

Harris Looms, North Grove Road, Hawkhurst, Kent.

The Hand Loom Centre, 59 Crest View Drive, Petts Wood, Kent.

Arrol Young, Netherdale, Galashiels, Scotland.

E. J. Arnold Ltd., Butterley Street, Leeds LS10 1AX.

Fleece:

Dryad, Northgates, Leicester.

Ebenezer Prior Ltd., Dyson Street, Bradford, Yorkshire.

Yarns:

Dryads, Northgates, Leicester.

Craftsman's Mark Ltd., Broadlands, Shortheath, Farnham, Surrey.

Handweavers' Studio and Gallery Ltd., 29 Haroldstone Road, London E17 7AN.

Hugh Griffiths, Brookdale, Beckington, Bath, Somerset.

T. M. Hunter, Sutherland Wool Mills, Brora, Sutherland. (Tweed yarns.)

J. Hyslop Bathgate & Co., Victoria Works, Galashiels, Scotland.

Weavers Shops Ltd., Wilton Royal Carpet Factory, Wilton, near Salisbury, Wilts. (6-ply and 2-ply rug wools and warp twine.)